ADVENTURES IN CULTURE

FOOD AROUND THE WORLD

By Charles Murphy

Gareth Stevens
PUBLISHING

Please visit our website, www.garethstevens.com. For a free color catalog of all our high-quality books, call toll free 1-800-542-2595 or fax 1-877-542-2596.

Cataloging-in-Publication Data

Names: Murphy, Charles.
Title: Food around the world / Charles Murphy.
Description: New York : Gareth Stevens Publishing, 2017. | Series: Adventures in culture| Includes index.
Identifiers: ISBN 9781482455823 (pbk.) | ISBN 9781482455847 (library bound) | ISBN 9781482455830 (6 pack)
Subjects: LCSH: Food habits–Juvenile literature. | Food–Juvenile literature. | Food habits–Cross-cultural studies.
Classification: LCC GT2850.M87 2017 | DDC 394.1'2 –dc23

Published in 2017 by
Gareth Stevens Publishing
111 East 14th Street, Suite 349
New York, NY 10003

Designer: Andrea Davison-Bartolotta and Bethany Perl
Editor: Therese Shea

Photo credits: Cover, p. 1 chinahbzyg/Shutterstock.com; pp. 2–24 (background texture) Flas100/Shutterstock.com; p. 5 Michael C. Gray/Shutterstock.com; p. 7 Vova Shevchuk/Shutterstock.com; p. 9 Blue Pig/Shutterstock.com; p. 11 Chad Zuber/Shutterstock.com; p. 13 Julie208/Shutterstock.com; p. 15 Dina Said/Wikipedia.org; p. 17 rocharibeiro/Shutterstock.com; p. 19 KucherAV/Shutterstock.com; p. 21 yasuhiro amano/Shutterstock.com.

Printed in China

CPSIA compliance information: Batch #CW17GS: For further information contact Gareth Stevens, New York, New York at 1-800-542-2595.

CONTENTS

Boldface words appear in the glossary.

Let's Eat!

What foods make your mouth water? Pizza? Your grandmother's macaroni and cheese? People around the world have foods they love, too. Some of those foods have a special meaning in their **culture**. Read on to find a new favorite **cuisine**!

In China

China has many cultures and cuisines. Rice and vegetables are common **ingredients**. Chinese who live **inland** often use hot peppers in their cooking. Peking duck is a famous dish from northern China. In the city of Beijing, people sell fried **scorpions**!

fried scorpion

In South Africa

African cuisine uses many vegetables. In South Africa, dried meat called biltong is sometimes made from ostrich or wild boar. Bobotie (buh-BOH-tee) is the national dish of South Africa. It's a pie made with meat, spices, sugar, milk, eggs, and fruit.

biltong

In Mexico

Mexican food often uses corn, beans, squash, and rice. Tacos, **tamales**, and burritos are found in many places. Flautas (FLOU-tuhz) are deep-fried, sugary treats made from flat bread. Some in southern Mexico eat chapulines (cha-poo-LEEN-ehs), which are fried grasshoppers!

chapulines

In Greece

The foods of Greece often include vegetables, fruits, olives, olive oil, cheese, bread, and seafood. A famous Greek baked dish is called moussaka (moo-SAH-kuh). It has eggplant, lamb, onions, tomatoes, cheese, and spices. Melopita, or honey pie, is a popular Greek **dessert**.

melopita

13

In Egypt

In Egypt, fava beans and spices are mashed into balls and fried. This is called falafel. Egyptians then make falafel sandwiches! Another favorite dish is koshari (koh-shah-REE). It contains **lentils**, macaroni, rice, tomatoes, onions, spices, and chickpeas.

koshari

In Brazil

Brazil is known for its steak houses. However, the Brazilian national dish is feijoada (fay-JWAH-duh), a stew of meats and beans served with rice and vegetables.

On the coast, Brazilians use shrimp they catch to make a stew called vatapá (vah-tah-PAH).

feijoada

In Australia

In Australia, native people called Aborigines have always eaten the meat of kangaroos and turtles. Meat pies are another popular dish. Vegemite (VEHJ-eh-myt) is a dark brown salty paste made from yeast products left over from making beer! It's often spread on bread.

meat pie

In Hawaii

Hawaii is known for poi, a bluish paste made of **taro** root. Poke (POH-kay) is a raw fish salad. Like other cultures, Hawaiians make tasty foods from the plants and animals around them. Which of these foods would you try?

poke

GLOSSARY

cuisine: food cooked in a certain way

culture: the beliefs and ways of life of a group of people

dessert: sweet food eaten after the main part of a meal

ingredient: a part of a mixture

inland: not near the coast or border

lentil: a seed that comes from a plant in the pea family

scorpion: a small animal related to spiders that has two front claws and a curved tail with a poisonous stinger at the end

tamale: a food that consists of seasoned ground meat or beans rolled in cornmeal, wrapped in a corn husk, and steamed

taro: a plant with a thick root that can be boiled and eaten

FOR MORE INFORMATION

BOOKS

Dodge, Abigail Johnson. *Around the World Cookbook*. New York, NY: DK Publishing, 2008.

Levete, Sarah. *Food Around the World*. Mankato, MN: Capstone Press, 2011.

Llanas, Sheila Griffin. *Easy Breakfasts from Around the World*. Berkeley Heights, NJ: Enslow Publishers, 2012.

WEBSITES

Food in Every Country
www.foodbycountry.com
Check out this amazing site to find a new favorite food.

International Recipes for Kids
www.easy-kids-recipes.com/international-recipes.html
Try making a dish from a different culture.

INDEX